TRANSCENDING RACE IN AMERICA
BIOGRAPHIES OF BIRACIAL ACHIEVERS

Halle Berry

Beyoncé

David Blaine

Mariah Carey

Frederick Douglass

W. E. B. Du Bois

Salma Hayek

Derek Jeter

Alicia Keys

Soledad O'Brien

Rosa Parks

Prince

Booker T. Washington

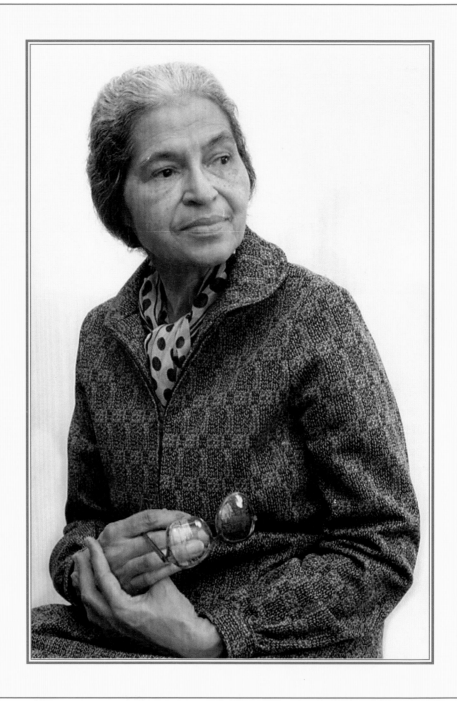

ROSA PARKS

Civil Rights Activist

Chuck Bednar

Mason Crest Publishers

Produced by 21st Century Publishing and Communications, Inc.

MASON CREST PUBLISHERS INC.
370 Reed Road
Broomall, Pennsylvania 19008
(866) MCP-BOOK (toll free)
www.masoncrest.com

Printed in the United States of America.

First Printing

9 8 7 6 5 4 3 2 1

Library of Congress Cataloging-in-Publication Data

Bednar, Chuck, 1976–
    Rosa Parks / Chuck Bednar.
       p. cm. — (Transcending race in America: biographies of biracial achievers)
    Includes bibliographical references and index.
    ISBN 978-1-4222-1615-6 (hardback : alk. paper) — ISBN 978-1-4222-1629-3 (pbk. : alk. paper)
    1. Parks, Rosa, 1913–2005—Juvenile literature. 2. African American women—Alabama—Montgomery—Biography—Juvenile literature. 3. African Americans—Alabama—Montgomery—Biography—Juvenile literature. 4. Civil rights workers—Alabama—Montgomery—Biography—Juvenile literature. 5. African Americans—Civil rights—Alabama—Montgomery—History—20th century—Juvenile literature. 6. Segregation in transportation—Alabama—Montgomery—History—20th century—Juvenile literature. 7. Montgomery (Ala.)—Race relations—Juvenile literature. 8. Montgomery (Ala.)—Biography—Juvenile literature. I. Title.
F334.M753P38238 2010
323.092—dc22
[B]   2009026370

Table of Contents

> *"I have brothers, sisters, nieces, nephews, uncles, and cousins, of every race and every hue, scattered across three continents, and for as long as I live, I will never forget that in no other country on Earth is my story even possible."*

> *"We may have different stories, but we hold common hopes. . . . We may not look the same and we may not have come from the same place, but we all want to move in the same direction — towards a better future . . ."*

— Barack Obama, 44th President of the United States of America

Standing Up
by Sitting Down

PULITZER PRIZE–WINNING POET RITA DOVE once wrote, "History is often portrayed as . . . all . . . heroics. Some of the most **tumultuous** events, however, have been provoked by **serendipity**." Such was certainly the case with Rosa Parks and the role she played in launching the civil rights movement in this country by simply staying in her seat.

In Rosa's hometown of Montgomery, Alabama, the custom in 1955 was for black bus passengers to pay at the front door, exit the bus, then re-enter through the back. Furthermore, the laws, called the Jim Crow Laws, required that, even if they were sitting in the "colored" section, they would have to give up their place if the "whites only" seats were full. The laws were grossly unfair, and Rosa knew it. After all, she had been ejected from the bus before for not following the rules.

Black passengers sit in the rear of a segregated bus in the 1950s in the South. According to the law, they had to give up their seats if the whites-only section filled up. In 1955 Rosa Parks stood up for her rights by staying in her seat, challenging the unfairness of the law.

TAKING THE FIRST STEP

On Thursday, December 1, Rosa boarded a bus on her way home from her job as a seamstress at a local Montgomery Fair department store. She had taken a seat in the fifth row, the first in the colored section, and all was well until the driver, J.P. Blake, ordered

Rosa and the other African Americans in that row to **relinquish** their seats to some white passengers who had just boarded. Rosa steadfastly refused. As she wrote in her 1994 book *Quiet Strength*:

> **❝Our mistreatment was not right, and I was tired of it. The more we gave in, the worse they treated us. . . . I knew someone had to take the first step. So I made up my mind not to move.❞**

Blake threatened to call the police if Rosa refused to move. Threats weren't about to scare her, though—she told him to do so. Approximately five minutes later, a pair of officers arrived at the scene. Blake pointed out where Rosa was sitting.

The two policemen went over to her and asked her why she refused to stand up. She replied that she didn't think she should have to. Then she asked one of the young men, "Why do you push us around?" He replied, "I don't know, but the law is the law, and you're under arrest." With that, Rosa was led off the bus and taken to jail.

The Start of Legalized Segregation

The Jim Crow Laws were a series of state and federals laws that were in effect starting in 1876. In essence, they marked the beginning of legalized **segregation**. The laws promised "separate but equal" facilities for black Americans, but in reality, the quality of the facilities provided was usually inferior.

Separate seating sections were established on buses and railway cars and in restaurants and theaters. Blacks had separate schools and hospitals. By the end of World War I, even places of employment had been segregated. The discrimination caused by the Jim Crow Laws lasted well into the 1900s.

NOT EASILY SHAKEN

Rosa was charged with disorderly conduct. She was photographed and fingerprinted, placed in a small room with bars, and ultimately moved to a larger cell that she shared with three other women. Rosa recalled in *Quiet Strength*,

Rosa was photographed like a criminal after she was arrested for refusing to give up her seat on December 1, 1955. She had decided to take the first step to end the mistreatment of blacks on the Montgomery bus system, which led to a citywide bus boycott.

> "Getting arrested was one of the worst days in my life. It was not a happy experience. . . . I felt very much alone . . . that I had been deserted. But I did not cry. I said a silent prayer and waited."

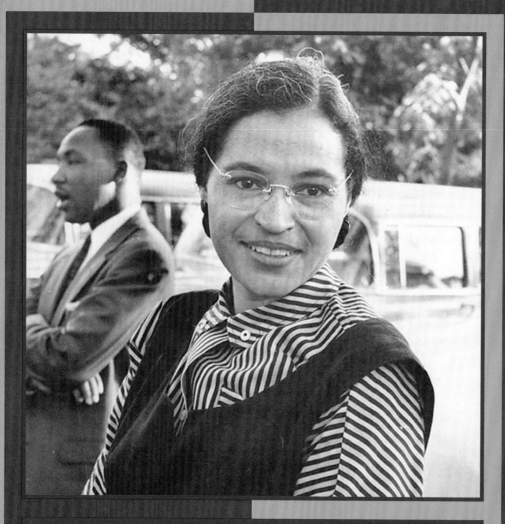

Rosa inspired Dr. Martin Luther King, Jr. (left) and others in the black community to begin organizing against discrimination. Although she didn't know it at the time, history would be changed forever because one day she did what she felt was right.

Eventually, her patience paid off. Rosa was released and allowed to return home. The day after she left jail, Rosa returned to work—much to the surprise of her co-workers, who she said "thought I would be too nervous and shaken to go back to work." As she had proved throughout the ordeal, though, Rosa Parks was not easily shaken.

SETTING THE WHEELS IN MOTION

While Rosa returned to her daily routine, behind the scenes, events had been set in motion that would change the world forever. Inspired by her actions, other members of the African-American community, including E.D. Nixon and Martin Luther King, Jr., realized that they could also actively rebel against racial oppression. Yet the woman who would be dubbed the "Mother of the Civil Rights Movement" never envisioned such an outcome when she refused to give up her seat on that fateful December day. Rosa recalled in her 1994 book,

> **I had no idea that history was being made. I was just tired of giving in. . . . I felt that what I did was right. . . . I did not think about the consequences.**

African Americans had dealt with the issues of slavery, segregation, and discrimination for a long time. Their history had been filled with tragedy, oppression, brutality, and bloodshed. Yet in the actions of Rosa Parks, they saw hope of a better day, where they could throw off the **shackles** of segregation, live free, and enjoy equality. U.S. Representative John Lewis of Georgia would tell CNN.com in 2005:

> **It was so unbelievable that this woman—this one woman—had the courage to take a seat and refuse to get up and give it up to a white gentleman. By sitting down, she was standing up for all Americans.**

African-American Oppression

THE AFRICAN-AMERICAN QUEST FOR freedom dates back hundreds of years, to the roots of slavery. In 1619, a Dutch ship brought approximately 20 African slaves to Jamestown, Virginia. The life of a slave was quite often **grueling** and extremely unpleasant. They worked hard, received no pay, had no rights, and were treated as their owner's property.

Although under the United States Constitution, slavery was not be banned nationwide until 1808, the Northwest Territory made slavery illegal in 1787. In 1808, Congress failed to ban slavery, but it did prohibit the importing of new slaves from Africa. In 1820, the Missouri Compromise banned slavery from the southern boundary of Missouri northward.

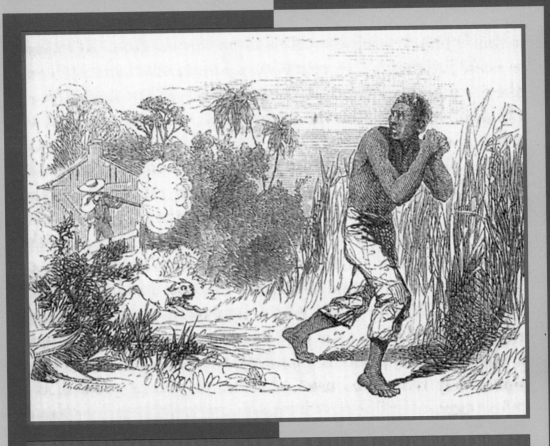

A slave owner shoots at a runaway slave. Slavery was in place for 200 years before being banned in some states. African Americans began organizing for legal freedom and equal rights in the 1800s, but they had a long way to go before achieving their goals.

EARLY CIVIL RIGHTS PIONEERS

History recalls blacksmith Gabriel Prosser as one of the very first champions of black civil rights. In 1800, Prosser organized a slave revolt that was to march on Richmond, Virginia. The plot was discovered, however, and Prosser and several others were hanged as a result. Others followed suit, including Denmark Vesey in South Carolina in 1822 and Nat Turner in Virginia in 1831. Each met a fate similar to Prosser's.

In 1831, William Lloyd Garrison began publishing an underground newspaper, *The Liberator*, which advocated the **abolition** of slavery. In 1849, former slave Harriet Tubman became one of the driving forces behind the Underground Railroad, which helped blacks who had escaped slavery reach safety. In 1852, Harriet Beecher Stowe published the famous anti-slavery novel *Uncle Tom's Cabin*. In 1868, future National Association for the Advancement of Colored People (NAACP) founder W.E.B. Du Bois was born.

W.E.B. Du Bois (front center facing right) poses with NAACP members in Cleveland, Ohio, in 1929. W.E.B. was an important protest leader who always spoke out for black rights. The NAACP, which he co-founded, still works to end racial discrimination.

The Father of the NAACP

William Edward Burghardt (W.E.B.) Du Bois was one of the most important black protest leaders of the 20th century. After graduating from Tennessee's Fisk University, Du Bois began work as a sociologist. Initially, he believed that he could discover the solution to the country's racial problems through research, but he later realized that activism would be required to enact change.

In 1905, Du Bois established the Niagara Movement, which eventually evolved into the NAACP. Du Bois became the NAACP's Director of Research and also edited the organization's official magazine. He left the NAACP in 1934, going on to write the books *Black Reconstruction* and *Dusk of Dawn*. Du Bois died in 1963, but the organization he helped to create remains influential to this day.

EMANCIPATION AND THE CIVIL WAR

While not the sole cause, slavery was certainly one of the primary issues that led to the conflict between the northern states and the southern ones, and ultimately, the Civil War. Seven southern states had seceded from the union by the time Abraham Lincoln became the 16th president of the United States in March 1861. By April, the first shots had been fired.

In 1863, Lincoln issued the Emancipation Proclamation, which declared that "all persons held as slaves . . . are, and shall henceforth be, free." It also opened the door for more than 200,000 freed southern blacks from the Confederacy to join the Union in the fight for their permanent freedom. According to the National Archives Web site:

> **From the first days of the Civil War, slaves had acted to secure their own liberty. The Emancipation Proclamation confirmed their insistence that the war for the Union must become a war for freedom. . . . As a milestone along the road to slavery's final destruction, the Emancipation Proclamation has assumed a place among the great documents of human freedom.**

Thanks largely to their efforts, the Civil War ended with a Union victory in 1865. Later that year, the Thirteenth Amendment to the Constitution officially abolished slavery in America.

"Separate but Equal"

On June 7, 1892, a man named Homer Plessy was arrested for sitting in the whites-only section of a Louisiana railway car. Actually, the 30-year-old Plessy was biracial, with one parent black and one white. But at the time, under Louisiana state law, he was considered black and as such could not use "white-only" facilities. The judge in the case, John Howard Ferguson, found him guilty.

Plessy appealed first to the Supreme Court of Louisiana, then to the U.S. Supreme Court, stating that his Thirteenth and Fourteenth Amendment rights had been violated. In the case of *Plessy* v. *Ferguson*, the Supreme Court ruled 7 to 1 against Plessy. The decision established the rule that separate facilities for different races was perfectly legal, as long as they were of equal quality. The ruling would stand until the 1950s.

NOT TRULY FREE

In a perfect world, the story would have ended there, but for African Americans, the fight had only just begun. They had officially gained their freedom, but they nonetheless still found themselves treated like second-class citizens. The 1896 decision handed down in the case of *Plessy* v. *Ferguson* essentially legalized segregation, and proved to be a setback towards the quest for equality that would last for decades.

As a result, the African-American community was forced to endure many years of inferior schools, subpar health care, and the threat of persecution for simply sitting next to a white person or using the same water fountain. More now than ever, they needed heroes to inspire them, and while men like Booker T. Washington and George Washington Carver were successful, many believe that it was Du Bois who best filled the role of civil rights champion.

In June 1905, a group led by the prominent black educator W.E.B. Du Bois met at Niagara Falls, Canada, sparking a new political protest movement to demand civil rights for blacks.

The Niagara Movement, as it was called, would soon be needed more than ever. Increases in population led to increases in unemployment, which led to increased racial hostilities. Race riots began breaking out, and in 1909, Du Bois and his Niagara Movement

The historical marker for the *Plessy* v. *Ferguson* case stands in New Orleans, Louisiana. The landmark 1896 decision legalized segregation and meant that blacks, even after becoming free men and women, were still considered inferior to whites. As a result, African-American leaders had to work even harder toward equality and civil rights.

supporters joined together to establish a permanent civil rights group, the NAACP. By 1921, the NAACP had branches in more than 400 U.S. cities. Their goals included the abolishment of segregation, equal educational opportunities for people of all races, and protection of the constitutional rights of African Americans.

The Tuskegee Airmen, an all-black air force battalion, were heroes during World War II. In the 1940s civil rights gained ground when the military was integrated. Black servicemen such as the Airmen showed the nation amazing bravery and patriotism, both in war and in the battle for racial equality.

GAINING GROUND

In 1925, civil rights leader A. Phillip Randolph created a predominantly African-American labor union, the Brotherhood of Sleeping Car Porters (BSCP). Randolph believed that black workers should band together and work for equality in the workplace. He and the BSCP, including a member named E.D. Nixon, would become major players in the early civil rights movement, especially in the Montgomery, Alabama area.

In 1941, Randolph threatened to organize a march on Washington, D.C., to push for desegregation of the military. The march was cancelled, though, when President Franklin Roosevelt issued the Fair Employment Act—the first national law to prohibit workplace discrimination. Many blacks became heroes during World War II, including Navy Cross recipient Dorie Miller and the Tuskegee Airmen, an all-black air force battalion that was awarded a Congressional Gold Medal in 2007. General Colin Powell, himself an African American, told the Airmen during that ceremony,

"You caused America to look in the mirror of its soul and you showed America that there was nothing a black person couldn't do."

Much progress had been made in the battle for equality, but there was still much to do. The battle for freedom may have ended with the Civil War and the Thirteenth Amendment, yet the war to end African-American oppression had only just begun. Against this backdrop, a future civil rights icon named Rosa Parks was born and raised.

Chapter

3

The Mother of Civil Rights

ALTHOUGH ROSA PARKS DID NOT BECOME a household name until her 1955 arrest, she was an active part of the civil rights movement throughout much of her life. Growing up, she learned to value family, education, dedication, freedom, and equality. As an adult, Rosa put those lessons into practice working on behalf of the African-American community.

Long before she became a civil rights crusader, Rosa Louise McCauley was born in Tuskegee, Alabama, on February 4, 1913. Her mother, Leona, was a schoolteacher. Her father, James, was a carpenter. Though she would become an inspiration to blacks, Rosa was actually of multiracial (African-American, Muscogee Indian, and Scots-Irish) ancestry. Early on in her life, James left the family to look for work. Rosa, her mother, and her younger brother, Sylvester, moved to her maternal grandparents' farm in Pine Level, Alabama.

Rosa's mother Leona (seated) poses with her cousin. Rosa's multiracial background included African Americans, Indians, and Scots-Irish settlers. Leona taught her daughter the value of education and dedication, which would later stand Rosa in good stead in her commitment to the civil rights cause.

GROWING UP WITH INJUSTICE

There, Rosa was raised by her mother and her grandparents, Rose and Sylvester Edwards. Both of Rosa's grandparents had been slaves raised during the Civil War era. She described grandma

Rose as "caring" and "strong-willed." Through her, Rosa developed a strong faith and a passion for reading the Bible. Grandpa Sylvester, meanwhile, was the child of a white **plantation** overseer and a black house slave. He often told Rosa stories of the mistreatment he had suffered. Rosa shared in her 1994 book:

> **"**He had . . . been cruelly treated by white people all his life. As a boy he had been beaten, forbidden to have shoes, and starved by the overseer of the plantation he lived on. . . . His memory will always be with me . . . my mother and I both learned not to let anyone mistreat us.**"**

Rosa was a sickly child, but when healthy, she attended the Montgomery Industrial School for Girls and the Alabama State Teachers College. She valued education and self-improvement, yet it seemed like **intolerance**, discrimination, and the threat of hate crimes lurked around every corner. Rosa wrote in *Quiet Strength*:

> **"**Fear was something very real for black people. . . . I saw and heard so much as a child growing up with hate and injustice . . . I set my mind to be a free person and not to give in to fear.**"**

BECOMING ACTIVE IN THE NAACP

In 1932, Rosa married Raymond Parks, a barber, a civil rights activist, and NAACP member. He was, in her words, "a good man, full of courage and inner strength . . . keenly interested in changing the current racial conditions." They moved to Montgomery, where Raymond worked tirelessly trying to free the Scottsboro Boys—nine young black men falsely accused of assaulting two white women.

In 1943, Rosa also became involved in the NAACP. She was elected secretary to the Montgomery branch's president, E.D. Nixon. According to the Academy of Achievement Web site, Rosa worked on "numerous" cases, but added:

"We didn't seem to have too many successes. It was more a matter of trying to challenge the powers that be, and to let it be known that we did not wish to continue being second-class citizens."

Quietly, Rosa and Raymond continued to quietly fight the good fight. Little did they know, though, that the battle against segregation was about to heat up.

Rosa (facing front) participates in a class discussion. She always believed in education and self-improvement and went to the Montgomery Industrial School for Girls and Alabama State Teachers College. Although she saw intolerance all around her, she never let discrimination keep her from her goals.

NAACP lawyers (from left) George Hayes, Thurgood Marshall, and James Nabrit celebrate outside the U.S. Supreme Court after winning the *Brown* v. *Board of Education* case in 1954. The court's decision was one of several rulings in the early 1950s that eliminated segregation in schools, the armed forces, and public transportation.

Montgomery's Civil Rights Champion

Born on July 12, 1899, Edgar Daniel Nixon only received a year of formal education. However, according to the Encyclopedia of Alabama Web site, he "had a natural ability to organize and to rally people around a cause." Throughout the 1940s, Nixon worked tirelessly to increase African-American voter registration in Montgomery.

In 1955, Nixon and Jo Ann Robinson, the president of the Women's Political Council, had been planning to launch a court challenge against segregation on Montgomery's public transport systems. Shortly thereafter, Nixon heard about Rosa's arrest. He met with her in jail and helped organize her bailout. Nixon died on February 25, 1987.

THE BATTLE FOR EQUALITY

In the 1950s, the civil rights movement started making headway. On June 5, 1950, the Supreme Court handed down three decisions against segregation. In one, the court forced the University of Texas to integrate its all-white law school. In another, they prohibited segregated seating on railroad dining cars.

In 1954, thanks to NAACP attorney Thurgood Marshall, the Supreme Court struck down segregation in schools in the case of *Brown* v. *Board of Education*. Marshall was a true hero of the early civil rights movement. He argued a total of 30 different civil rights cases before the U.S. Supreme Court, winning all but one. Years later Harvard Law Professor Laurence Tribe told *Time* magazine in 1991,

> **"He is truly a living legend. It is hard to think of another lawyer in the 20th century who has played a more important role."**

Battles were being won in other ways as well. In 1951, the New York City Council passed a bill prohibiting racial discrimination. In 1954, the U.S. Defense Department eliminated all segregated units in the armed forces. Then, in 1955, the Interstate Commerce Commission ruled that segregated seating on buses that traveled across state lines violated the Interstate Commerce Act.

Brown v. Board of Education

In 1951, the parents of 20 Topeka, Kansas, school children filed a class-action lawsuit against the city, seeking to do away with a policy allowing school districts to establish separate schools based on race. One **plaintiff**, Oliver Brown, was an African-American welder and pastor whose daughter walked six blocks to catch a bus to a blacks-only school each day.

Eventually, the U.S. Supreme Court chose to hear the case. In a unanimous decision, they ruled that "separate educational facilities are **inherently** unequal" and violated the Fourteenth Amendment. Though many people were unhappy with the decision, and the transition was not a smooth one, *Brown* v. *Board of Education* opened the door for racial integration in schools.

ROSA AND HER PREDECESSORS

In the months prior to Rosa's arrest, several other African Americans had been arrested for refusing to give up their bus seats to white passengers. In March, 15-year-old Claudette Colvin was jailed for failing to relinquish her seat. Alabama State University graduate Aurelia Browder was arrested on similar charges in April. Later, so were two other women—Mary Louise Smith and Susie McDonald.

Colvin was a high school student and part of the NAACP Youth Council when she was arrested. The Congress of Racial Equality Web site reports that she was approached by two officers. One allegedly kicked her, while the other knocked the textbooks she was carrying out of her hands and onto the floor. Claudette was handcuffed, brutally dragged off the bus, and thrown in jail. She later said that she wasn't disappointed with her relative obscurity.

❝I feel proud of what I did . . . what I did was a spark and it caught on. . . . Let the people know Rosa Parks was the right person for the boycott. But also let them know that the attorneys took four other women to the Supreme Court to challenge the law that led to the end of segregation.❞

Before Rosa's arrest, several other black women had "mug shots" taken after being charged with refusing to give up their seats to white passengers. Although they were not happy at the time, they were equally proud of their brave acts and contributions to the Civil Rights Movement.

Nixon and the NAACP had been looking for a person through whom they could challenge Montgomery's segregation laws. For some reason, though, Claudette and the others were considered wrong for the part. However, on December 1, 1955, highly respected 42-year-old Rosa Parks was also arrested for refusing to surrender her seat to a white passenger. Little did she know that she was about to become "The Mother of the Civil Rights Movement."

Chapter

4

❀

Boycotts, Trials, and Victories

BY 1955, AFRICAN AMERICANS HAD CON-tributed much to the world. They had proved they could excel as athletes, scientists, politicians, diplomats, entertainers, and soldiers. Yet, as the arrest of Rosa Parks illustrated, they could still be jailed for simply failing to surrender their bus seats to white passengers. The black citizens of Montgomery, Alabama, had finally had enough.

Immediately after Rosa's arrest, E.D. Nixon and Jo Ann Robinson of the Women's Political Council (WPC) set to work organizing a boycott of the Montgomery buses. Robinson spent the night creating thousands of fliers asking African Americans to stay off the city buses in protest of Rosa's treatment. The document, which was published in the *Montgomery Advertiser* newspaper on Sunday, December 4, read:

Rosa and E.D. Nixon (left), leader of the NAACP in Alabama, arrive at court in Montgomery, Alabama, in 1956. Always a leader in the quest for civil rights, Nixon worked to bail Rosa out of jail, challenge the segregation laws, and organize the bus boycott.

"Another Negro woman has been arrested and thrown into jail because she refused to get up out of her seat on the bus and give it to a white person. . . . This must be stopped. Negroes are citizens and have rights. . . . Until we do something to stop these arrests they will continue. . . . We are, therefore, asking every Negro to stay off the buses on Monday in protest of the arrest and trial."

On December 5, Rosa's trial took place. It took less than an hour. She was found guilty and forced to pay a $10 fine, plus $4 in court costs. Meanwhile, despite rainy weather, the bus boycott was a tremendous success. Nearly 90 percent of the city's black population carpooled, took cabs, or walked to work.

THE MONTGOMERY BUS BOYCOTT

The work had just begun, though. Later that day, thousands of African Americans met at Holt Street Baptist Church. The Montgomery Improvement Agency (MIA) was formed, and Rev. Martin Luther King, Jr. was elected president.

Although originally the bus boycott was supposed to last only one day, it continued throughout December and into 1956. During this time, the MIA met with Montgomery city leaders and bus company officials, trying to work out a revised seating plan that would be fairer to black passengers. In the meantime, the MIA began a massive carpool operation. One of the lead organizers of the effort was a white pastor named Robert S. Graetz. In a story published in the *Montgomery Advertiser* on January 10, 1956, he said:

> "Sometime ago I read that the first requisite of a successful missionary was that he become color blind. I figured that the same was true of my work here. . . . I know that I shall be criticized for my stand. I may ever suffer violence. But I cannot minister to souls alone. My people also have bodies."

By the end of January, negotiations had broken down, and at the urging of attorney Fred D. Gray, the MIA voted to file a federal lawsuit against Montgomery mayor W.A. Gayle. Then the dispute turned violent. King's house was bombed on January 30, and Nixon's on February 1. No one was injured, and fortunately, King was able to talk angry African Americans out of responding with violence of their own. In February 1956, Gray and Charles D. Langford filed suit on behalf of Rosa Parks and the four other women who were similarly arrested.

Black residents of Montgomery, Alabama, walk everywhere as part of the 1956 bus boycott. Rev. Martin Luther King, Jr. led the movement through legal struggles and other challenges. After more than a year, the boycott ended after the Supreme Court outlawed segregation on Alabama buses.

Rosa is fingerprinted after being charged with organizing the boycott in Montgomery, Alabama, in 1956. As a result of her efforts and those of activists like Martin Luther King, Jr., the boycott was a huge success. Almost 90 percent of black citizens avoided the buses and walked or carpooled to work.

VICTORY IN MONTGOMERY

As the case prepared to go to court, the boycott continued, and the battle grew fiercer. In late February, 90 organizers were indicted on charges of violating a law prohibiting boycotts without just

a sits in the front of a Montgomery bus after segregation was ruled illegal
he city's bus system. Behind Parks is a white reporter covering the event.
a was proud to have been part of a movement that was a landmark in the
ggle for civil rights.

A NEW LEADER RISES

ring the Montgomery Bus Boycott, Martin Luther King, Jr. had
played tremendous leadership and character. As a result, he soon
nd himself at the forefront of the entire civil rights movement.
sa first met Dr. King during the early stages of the boycott. Even
ugh he was many years her junior (she was 42; he was 26),
rtin left a lasting impression. Rosa recalled in *Quiet Strength*:

> "Dr. King was a true leader. I never sensed fear in
> him . . . he knew what had to be done and took the
> leading role without regard to consequences. I knew
> he was destined to do great things."

cause. In April, African Americans were denied a permi[...]
allow them to run a bus service for blacks only. Later[...]
who used their motor vehicles for carpools suddenly [...]
denied insurance policies.

All the while, the U.S. Supreme Court had b[...]
arguments in the case of *Browder* v. *Gayle*. In Nov[...]
reached a unanimous decision. Laws requiring se[...]
Alabama buses were unconstitutional. On Decer[...]
order to integrate the buses became official, and th[...]
to end the bus boycott.

The Case that Overthrew Segregation

I n 1956, the U.S. District Court in Alabama heard the case of *Browder* v. *Gayle*, which challenged the legality of Montgomery's bus segregation laws. Along with Rosa Parks, Alabama State University graduate Aurelia Browder was a plaintiff in the case. Montgomery mayor W.A. Gayle was named as the **defendant**.

After hearing legal arguments from both sides, the court ruled that "enforced segregation of N[...]
gers on motor bu[...]
of Montgomery [...]
and laws of the U[...]
effectively put a[...]
the city buses i[...]
black residents[...]
find themselves[...]
discrimination or[...]
to come.

Martin Luther King, Jr. called the victory a "gl[...]
to end a long night of enforced segregation."[...]
vowed she would never step foot on a segregated[...]
being arrested, took her first integrated bus ride [...]
boycott ended. For Rosa, the victory was especi:[...]
wrote later,

66 During the Montgomery bus boyco[...]
together and remained unified for 381[...]
never been done again. The Montgom[...]
became the model for human rights [...]
the world. 99

King and his wife, Coretta, moved to Montgomery in 1954. He intended on serving as the pastor for the Dexter Avenue Baptist Church. After Rosa's arrest, however, he was handpicked by Jo Ann Robinson to become the face of the boycott efforts. According to Jannell McGrew of the *Montgomery Advertiser*, Robinson wanted "an energetic leader with a presence, someone who could peacefully rally leaders and residents together for one cause."

The boycott ended in late 1956, but King's role as a civil rights leader was only just beginning. In 1957, he helped create the Southern Christian Leadership Conference (SCLC), which was established to help organize African-American churches together and promote civil rights reform through nonviolent means. Just

Martin Luther King, Jr. (center wearing dark suit) stands outside the Montgomery courthouse with other black activists in 1956. As a result of the bus boycott he took a leading role in the civil rights movement. Rosa recognized his power as a leader and knew he was meant for greatness.

as Rosa Parks is often referred to as the "Mother of Civil Rights" for her part in the movement, King is known as one of the true fathers of civil rights for the many great things he accomplished during his life.

The King of Civil Rights

Born on January 15, 1929, Martin Luther King, Jr. was a Baptist minister and civil rights activist who earned a doctorate degree in systematic theology from Boston University in 1955. Later that year, he led the Montgomery Bus Boycott, and in 1957, he co-founded the Southern Christian Leadership Conference (SCLC).

King preached the use of nonviolent techniques to advance the cause. Through the use of marches and protests, he fought for civil rights in Alabama, Georgia, and Florida during the early to mid 1960s. In 1964, Martin became the youngest person ever to receive the Nobel Peace Prize. Following his assassination in 1968, he was awarded the Presidential Medal of Freedom in 1977 and the Congressional Gold Medal in 2004. A national holiday was established in his honor in 1986.

CIVIL RIGHTS IN THE EARLY '60S

In 1957—the same year in which the SCLC was formed and President Dwight Eisenhower sent U.S. army soldiers to Little Rock, Arkansas, to enforce integration in schools—Rosa and her husband Raymond moved to Detroit, Michigan. She had lost her seamstress job the previous year when that Montgomery Fair location closed its tailor shop. Soon after, she left to work for two years at Virginia University, before returning to Detroit in 1959 and opening a sewing factory there in 1961.

Meanwhile, the 1960s also brought changes and new developments to the civil rights movement. Sit-ins, which involved large groups of people occupying a particular space to block access to a specific location, became the favored form of nonviolent protest. The first notable sit-in occurred in February 1960 in Greensboro, North Carolina. Four North Carolina A&T freshmen (Ezell Blair, Jr., David Richmond, Joseph McNeil, Franklin McCain) were denied service at a lunch counter in a Woolworth's department store.

The next day, they returned with over two dozen others to occupy seats at the counter. The day after that, the total number of people involved topped 60, and by February 5, more than 300 students were taking part in the protest. Eventually, sit-ins started in other locations, and by July 26, Woolworth stores were officially desegregated. The success of the sit-ins would spawn other similar, equally as successful campaigns throughout the decade.

On August 28, 1963, Dr. King, BSCP founder A. Phillip Randolph, Congress of Racial Equality President James Farmer, Student Nonviolent Coordinating Committee president John Lewis, NAACP president Roy Wilkins, and National Urban League president Whitney Young organized the March on Washington for

Martin Luther King, Jr. greets the crowd before giving his famous "I Have a Dream" speech during the 1963 March on Washington. He was an advocate of nonviolent protests and inspired sit-ins that spread across the south and led to the rally in Washington in support of racial equality.

Jobs and Freedom. The March was a political rally, attended by over 200,000 people, that advocated freedom, workplace equality, and racial harmony. Rosa was among those in attendance at the rally as King gave his now legendary "I Have a Dream" speech.

"I Have a Dream"

On August 28, 1963, a group of between 200,000 and 300,000 men and women, led by Martin Luther King, Jr., held a political rally in Washington, D.C. The march started at the Washington Monument and ended at the Lincoln Memorial, and featured several guest speakers, though none made a greater impact than King.

During the rally, Martin gave his famous "I Have a Dream" speech, in which he discussed his vision of an America where people of all races could live in harmony and enjoy equality. The powerful message is perhaps best summed up by an excerpt from the speech:

> 66 I have a dream that my four little children will one day live in a nation where they will not be judged by the color of their skin, but by the content of their character. 99

SURVIVING BLOODY SUNDAY

Rosa also was a part of the 1965 Selma to Montgomery Marches. Through the 1950s and early 1960s, there had been a series of concentrated efforts to keep African Americans from voting. On July 6, 1964, Lewis and about 50 others were arrested while attempting to register to vote. Dr. King and the SCLC were called in, and his speech on January 2, 1965, officially kicked off what became known as the Selma Voting Rights Movement.

The first of the three marches took place on March 7, 1965. More than 600 civil rights activists were attacked by state and local law enforcement en route to Montgomery. One person was killed, 17 were hospitalized, and countless others were left bruised and beaten in what became known as "Bloody Sunday." The second march was to be held two days later, on March 9, but after Bloody Sunday, a court order was issued prohibiting the civil rights activists from traveling all the way to Montgomery.

Martin Luther King, Jr. leads the third Selma to Montgomery voting rights march in 1965. After an earlier march ended in violence, participants were nervous to try again. But Rosa and other activists joined Martin, and more than 8,000 people successfully marched to Selma.

On March 18, a court ruled that King and the other activists had the right, under the First Amendment, to march from Selma to Montgomery. Three days later, Martin, Rosa, and roughly 8,000 others began a five-day, four-night march that culminated with a Stars for Freedom rally featuring performers such as Harry Belafonte, Tony Bennett, and Sammy Davis, Jr.

SUCCESS AT LAST

The struggles and sacrifices of the African-American civil rights community over the years had been almost too much to imagine. By the mid-1960s, though, all their hard work began to bear fruit. In 1964, Congress passed Public Law 82-352, better known as the Civil Rights Act of 1964. The new law prohibited discrimination

President Lyndon B. Johnson signs the 1964 Civil Rights Act as Martin Luther King, Jr. (standing center) and others look on. The law banned racial and gender discrimination and was the direct result of the efforts of civil rights activists like Rosa. Victory and equal rights had come at last.

on the basis of race or gender, and as the Center for American Progress notes on its Web site, it was a landmark victory for the civil rights movement.

> **"The Act indelibly changed life in America. 'Whites only' water fountains, pools and restaurants became illegal, and 'no blacks need apply' job announcements became a violation of federal law. [It] provided a major tool in the desegregation of hospitals, nursing homes, and other health care facilities."**

The following year, Congress passed the Voting Rights Act of 1965. This law outlawed discriminatory voting practices, including anything that would "deny . . . the right of any citizen of the United States to vote on account of race or color." According to fellow SCLC activist C.T. Vivian, Dr. King quietly sat in a chair with a tear running down his cheek as he first learned of the bill's passing. It was truly a glorious day for the civil rights movement.

In 1965, Rosa Parks returned to Detroit, where she went to work for newly elected Congressman John Conyers. The two shared many similar goals. Both strived to work for civil rights, and according to John Nichols of thenation.com, both also worked for "peace, economic justice, and an end to the death penalty." Rosa's time in the spotlight might have come to an end, but her work for the good of African Americans was far from over.

Chapter

5

❈

A Timeless Legacy

ROSA PARKS WAS THE CATALYST FOR THE events that led to many civil rights gains in the 1950s and 1960s. However, by 1970, she had left the Montgomery Bus Boycott era behind her. Rosa was now hard at work as an aide in John Conyers' Detroit office, helping the African-American representative as he continued the civil rights fight in Congress.

Conyers accomplished much on that front. The congressman was a founding member of the Congressional Black Caucus, a group representing African Americans in the governing body. Furthermore, following Dr. King's assassination in 1968, Conyers began working to honor the late civil rights leader with a national holiday—work that would not reach its successful conclusion until many, many years later. Years later Conyers told *Democracy Now* that he was honored to have Rosa's support along the way:

In the 1970s, Rosa lived in Detroit and was an aide to a congressman who still worked toward civil rights. No one had forgotten her contribution to the bus boycott, though, and the NAACP gave her an award for her outstanding lifetime achievements.

Rosa (center) stands on the steps of the Dexter Avenue Baptist Church in Montgomery, Alabama, with civil rights leaders Ralph Abernathy (top) and Coretta Scott King, Martin Luther King's widow. On December 5, 1975, they all celebrated the 20th anniversary of Rosa's refusal to give up her bus seat.

> **“**I said that when I won this seat, the first thing I would do is offer her a position on my staff, if she would accept. And to my honor and delight, she did accept. . . . I can't help but marvel at the fact that Rosa Parks essentially had a saint-like quality . . . she never raised her voice. She was not an emotional person in terms of expressing anger or rage or vindictiveness. But she was **resolute.”**

In 1975, Rosa celebrated the 20th anniversary of the Montgomery Bus Boycott, and in 1979, the NAACP awarded her its highest honor: the Spingarn Medal. Sadly, though, she would also suffer many tragedies throughout the decade. In 1977, her husband, Raymond, died of cancer. Later that year, her brother, Sylvester, passed as well. Then two years later, she lost her mother, Leona. A devout member of the African Methodist Episcopal Church, Rosa turned to her faith to help her through these difficult hardships, and through God, she found the strength to carry on.

WORKING FOR THE PEOPLE

In 1980, the *Detroit News* and Detroit public schools announced the creation of the Rosa L. Parks Scholarship Foundation. According to the group's official Web site, the goal of the foundation is to award scholarships to high school seniors throughout Michigan who "hold close to Mrs. Parks' ideals while demonstrating academic skills, community involvement, and economic need." Through June 2009, more than 800 students have been granted over $1.6 million in foundation scholarships.

During the month of February, 1987, Rosa and longtime friend Elaine Steele co-founded the Rosa and Raymond Parks Institute for Self-Development. Regarding the establishment of the Institute, Rosa had this to say:

> **“**Children are my passion and I believe that everyone can make a difference in their lives. Our young people are curious, eager to learn, and need the guidance of

mentors who care about their development. After all, they are our future and we must someday depend on their leadership. We hope to encourage an environment of dignity, responsibility, and a commitment to treat others as we wish to be treated. **,,**

The following year, Rosa stepped down from her position in Congressman Conyers' office. She was now in her 70s, and had spent decades working for the public good. Thus, many assumed that she was ending her lifelong work. As she pointed out in *Quiet Strength*, though, they were wrong. "I never thought that job as a retirement from life," she wrote. "I just felt that I now had more time to do more of my work for the people."

COMING FULL CIRCLE

True to her word, Rosa remained active throughout the rest of her life, and received numerous honors for her work as well. Following his release from prison in 1990, African civil rights activist Nelson Mandela personally asked to meet with her, telling Rosa that she was an inspiration to him in the fight against segregation in his homeland. In 1991, the Smithsonian Institution in Washington, D.C., unveiled a bust in her image. The following year, her first book, *Rosa Parks: My Story*, was published by Dial Books.

Rosa received a pair of honors in 1994. First, she was granted an honorary degree from Soka University in Japan, and then she received the Rosa Parks Peace Prize, named in her honor, in Stockholm, Sweden. Later that year, she completed her second book, a volume of memories and inspirational thoughts entitled *Quiet Strength: The Faith, the Hope, and the Heart of a Woman Who Changed a Nation*.

In 1996, President Bill Clinton presented Rosa with the Medal of Freedom, the highest civilian honor that can be granted by the chief executive. Two years later, *Time* magazine named her one of the 100 Most Important People of the Century, and in 1999, Congress bestowed upon her the Congressional Gold Medal. On

December 1, 2000, Troy University in Montgomery broke ground on the Rosa Parks Memorial Library and Museum. The facility was located at the exact corner where her 1955 arrest had taken place, thus bringing her story full circle.

Rosa is greeted by Vice President Al Gore during her Congressional Gold Medal ceremony in Detroit, November 28, 1999. She kept active throughout her later life, writing books and receiving numerous honors for her work, both in the U.S. and overseas.

The Highest Honor

The Congressional Gold Medal, which is presented by the United States Congress, is one of the highest honors that can be awarded to a civilian. Both houses of Congress, the House of Representatives and the Senate, must approve the awarding of the honor by a two-thirds margin. A unique medal is then created by the U.S. Mint and presented to the recipient.

Over the years, many famous historical figures, entertainers, authors, pioneers, scientists, athletes, and humanitarians have been presented with the Congressional Gold Medal. They include George Washington, the Wright Brothers, Thomas Edison, Dr. Jonas Salk, Walt Disney, John Wayne, Harry S. Truman, Mother Teresa, Pope John Paul II, *Peanuts* creator Charles Schultz, and composer Irving Berlin.

THE PASSING OF AN ICON

Rosa Parks died in Detroit, Michigan, on October 24, 2005. She was 92. Though she had reportedly suffered from dementia, failing health, and financial difficulties later in life, she continued making public appearances until the end. Her funeral was held on November 2, 2005, at St. Paul African Methodist Episcopal Church in Montgomery. More than 4,000 people attended the service, paying their respects and remembering the life and legacy of "The Mother of Civil Rights" during a service lasting more than seven hours.

Her coffin was brought to the chapel in a gray and white horse-drawn carriage, followed by 15 white limousines filled with some of her dearest friends. During the service, then-Illinois Senator Barack Obama was among those who paid tribute to her life, her legacy, and her contributions to the civil rights movement. During his speech, Obama said,

"The woman we honored today held no public office, she wasn't a wealthy woman, didn't appear in the society pages. And yet when the history of this country is written, it is this small, quiet woman whose name will be remembered long after the names of senators and presidents have been forgotten."

At Rosa's funeral in 2005, friends, politicians, dignitaries, and thousands of ordinary people joined to honor her life and her legacy. Among the speakers was a senator named Barack Obama, who said the country would never forget her contributions to the civil rights movement.

Also among those on hand were singer Aretha Franklin, politicians Jesse Jackson and Al Sharpton, former president Bill Clinton, Secretary of State Condoleezza Rice, and Rev. Bernice King (daughter of Martin Luther King, Jr.). Detroit mayor Kwame Kilpatrick said of Rosa, "Thank you for sacrificing for us. . . . Thank you for allowing us to step on your mighty shoulders." At the end of the service, an American flag was unfolded onto Rosa's casket, and the tireless civil rights pioneer was laid to rest.

THE LEGACY OF ROSA PARKS

On December 1, 2005, less than a month after her funeral, the nation celebrated the 50th anniversary of her legendary act of defiance. The day was declared "National Transit Tribute to Rosa Parks Day," and in Montgomery, Alabama, special banners and seat signs in her honor were placed on all of the city buses. The cemetery where she and her husband were buried was renamed the Rosa L. Parks Freedom Chapel, and President George W. Bush signed into law a bill that would place a statue of her in the U.S. Capitol. During that ceremony, President Bush said:

> **"By refusing to give in, Rosa Parks showed that one candle can light the darkness. . . . By refusing to give in, Rosa Parks helped inspire a nationwide effort for equal justice under the law. . . . By refusing to give in, Rosa Parks called America back to its founding promise of equality and justice for everyone. . . . Rosa Parks helped her fellow African Americans claim their God-given freedoms and made America a better place."**

Rosa's legacy lives on in other ways as well. Her actions helped open the door for other civil rights leaders, including Martin Luther King, Jr., and through their actions many African Americans were able to seize opportunities previously unavailable to them. In many ways, what she started, and what King continued, was ultimately fulfilled through Barack Obama's successful 2008 presidential campaign. Even then, Rosa's name was a rallying cry—one that would help carry Obama into the White House. Jose Antonio Vargas of washingtonpost.com pointed out:

> **"'Rosa sat so Martin could walk. Martin walked so Barack could run. Barack is running so our children can fly.' That 86-letter text message is being forwarded from cellphone to cellphone. It began among African**

Americans then went viral, posted in various blogs. Exactly when it was first sent, who sent it and how many times it has been forwarded, we don't know. **"**

Rosa's face appears on a wall mural with Martin Luther King and Barack Obama in Los Angeles. The journey she began, followed by the deeds of activists like Martin, created more opportunities for African Americans, and ultimately led to the election of President Obama.

Rosa's life is remembered in a wax figure display at Madame Tussauds Museum in Washington, D.C. Her dedication to the civil rights movement was important and inspiring. But her simple wish was to be remembered as someone who just wanted freedom for herself and others.

The First Biracial President

Born on August 4, 1961, Barack Hussein Obama is a graduate of Columbia University. After graduating from Columbia, he worked as a community organizer in Chicago for a while before he enrolled in Harvard Law School, where he worked hard and became the first black president of the prestigious Harvard Law Review. After graduation from Harvard he returned to Chicago where he worked as a civil rights attorney. He also taught constitutional law at the University of Chicago from 1992 through 2004. In 1997, Barack ran for and won a seat in the Illinois State Senate, where he remained until he ran for the United States Senate in 2004.

Thanks largely to his keynote speech at the Democratic National Convention that summer, he won the election by the largest margin in his home state's history. In February 2007, he announced he would run for the office of president of the United States in 2008. Obama received the Democratic nomination and defeated Arizona Senator John McCain to become the first biracial president in United States history.

REMEMBERING ROSA PARKS

The life of Rosa Parks was filled with courage, hard work, dedication, and faith. She had stood up for herself by remaining seated on that Montgomery bus in 1955. In doing so, she ignited a movement that would bring civil rights into the 20th century. When she was writing her second book in 1994, she discussed what her legacy should be. Rosa said,

> **"I want to be remembered as a person who stood up to injustice, who wanted a better world for young people; and most of all, I want to be remembered as a person who wanted to be free and wanted others to be free."**

1619   The first African slaves are brought to the United States.

1861   Abraham Lincoln is elected President, and the Civil War begins.

1863   Lincoln issues the Emancipation Proclamation, declaring that "all persons held as slaves . . . are, and shall henceforth be, free."

1865   The Civil War ends, and the Thirteenth Amendment bans slavery in the United States.

1892   In the case of *Plessy* v. *Ferguson*, the Supreme Court rules that the creation of "separate but equal" facilities for blacks and whites is constitutional, effectively legalizing segregation.

1909   The National Association for the Advancement of Colored People (NAACP) is co-founded by W.E.B. Du Bois.

1913   Rosa Louise McCauley is born in Tuskegee, Alabama, on February 4.

1932   Rosa marries NAACP activist Raymond Parks on December 18.

1943   Rosa becomes involved with the NAACP as she is elected secretary for Montgomery branch president E.D. Nixon.

1949   Rosa becomes an adviser to the NAACP Youth Council.

1954   In the case of *Brown* v. *Board of Education*, the Supreme Court rules that "separate educational facilities are inherently unequal," thus opening the door for racial integration in schools.

1955   Rosa meets Dr. Martin Luther King, Jr.

On December 1, she is arrested in Montgomery, Alabama, for refusing to give up her bus seat to a white passenger.

Four days later, the Montgomery Bus Boycott begins.

1956   On February 1, Fred D. Gray and Charles D. Langford file a lawsuit against Montgomery mayor W.A. Gayle on behalf of Rosa Parks.

Nine months later, the Supreme Court overturns segregation laws on buses, and in December, the boycott ends with the integration of buses.

1957   Dr. Martin Luther King, Jr. helps establish the Southern Christian Leadership Conference.

Rosa moves to Detroit, Michigan.

1963   Rosa participates in the March on Washington, where Dr. King delivers his famous "I Have a Dream" speech.

1965   Rosa participates in the Selma to Montgomery Marches.

Later, she begins working as an aide to Congressman John Conyers.

1977   Rosa's husband, Raymond, and brother, Sylvester, die.

1979   Rosa is awarded the NAACP's Spingarn Medal.

Rosa's mother, Leona, passes away.

1980   The Rosa L. Parks Scholarship Foundation is established.

1987   The Rosa and Raymond Parks Institute for Self-Development is founded.

1988   Rosa retires from her position in Congressman Conyers' office.

1992   Her first book, *Rosa Parks: My Story*, is published by Dial Books.

1996   President Bill Clinton presents her with the Presidential Medal of Freedom.

1998   *Time* magazine names Rosa one of the 100 Most Important People of the Century.

1999   Congress presents her with the Congressional Gold Medal.

2005   Rosa Parks dies on October 24, and is laid to rest on November 2.

On December 1, the country celebrates the 50th anniversary of the Montgomery Bus Boycott, and President George W. Bush signs a law allowing a statue of her likeness to be placed in the U.S. Capitol.

2008   The country's first biracial president, Barack Obama, is elected.

Awards

1979   NAACP Spingarn Medal

1980   Martin Luther King, Jr. Award

           Martin Luther King, Jr. Nonviolent Peace Prize

           Ebony Service Award

1984   Eleanor Roosevelt Women of Courage Award

1986   Medal of Honor

1987   Martin Luther King, Jr. Leadership Award

1990   Adam Clayton Powell , Jr. Legislative Achievement Award

1994   Rosa Parks Peace Prize, Stockholm, Sweden

1996   Presidential Medal of Freedom

1999   Congressional Gold Medal

2000   Alabama Governor's Medal for Extraordinary Courage

Accomplishments

1955   Participates in the Montgomery Bus Boycott.

1963   Participates in the March on Washington.

1965   Participates in the the Selma to Montgomery Marches.

1980   Rosa L. Parks Scholarship Foundation established.

1987   Rosa and Raymond Parks Institute for Self-Development founded.

1998   Named one of the 100 Most Important People of the Century by *Time* Magazine.

2000   Rosa Parks Memorial Library and Museum, Troy University is established.

2005   December 1 is named National Transit Tribute to Rosa Parks Day.

Rosa L. Parks Freedom Chapel is established.

Statue of Rosa Parks is placed in the U.S. Capitol.

Books

1992   *Rosa Parks: My Story* (with Jim Haskins)

1994   *Quiet Strength: The Faith, the Hope, and the Heart of a Woman Who Changed a Nation* (with Gregory J. Reed)

1996   *Dear Mrs. Parks: A Dialogue with Today's Youth*

1997   *I Am Rosa Parks* (with Jim Haskins)

abolition—doing away with something, often used in reference to slavery.

catalyst—a person or thing that causes an important change to occur.

defendant—a person accused of a crime.

grueling—very difficult, or full of hardships.

inherently—existing as an essential characteristic.

intolerance—unwillingness or inability to accept differences in people or things.

relinquish—give up or surrender.

resolute—determined, brave, courageous, and decisive.

plantation—a large farm or estate, usually run by resident workers.

plaintiff—the person who files a lawsuit in court.

segregation—separation based on race or ethnic group.

serendipity—the act of accidentally discovering something beneficial, while not actively looking for it. Finding a pleasant surprise.

shackles—a physical restraint used on the wrists or ankles; sometimes used as a metaphor to describe oppression or anything that restricts freedom.

tumultuous—troubled, difficult, or disruptive.

Books and Periodicals

Hull, Mary. *Rosa Parks: Civil Rights Leader*. New York: Chelsea House, 2007.

Parks, Rosa. *Dear Mrs. Parks: A Dialogue With Today's Youth*. New York: Lee & Low Books, 1996.

Parks, Rosa and Gregory J. Reed. *Quiet Strength: The Faith, the Hope, and the Heart of a Woman who Changed a Nation*. Grand Rapids, Michigan: Zondervan, 1994.

Parks, Rosa and Jim Haskins. *I Am Rosa Parks*. New York: Puffin Books, 1997.

Parks, Rosa and Jim Haskins. *Rosa Parks: My Story*. New York: Dial Books, 1992.

Wilson, Camilla. *Rosa Parks: From the Back of the Bus to the Front of a Movement*. New York: Scholastic, 2001.

Web Sites

http://www.rosaparks.org/

The official Web site of the Rosa & Raymond Parks Institute for Self Development, which was founded by the civil rights pioneer in 1987. The site contains a bio and timeline of Rosa's life, as well as information about the Institute's programs, videos, and much more.

http://www.montgomeryboycott.com/frontpage.htm

This Web site, owned and operated by the *Montgomery Advertiser* newspaper, contains in-depth coverage of the Montgomery Bus Boycott. It includes 1955-era news stories, bios of Rosa Parks and the other principle figures involved, voice clips, and more.

http://www.e-portals.org/Parks/

The Rosa Parks Portal is an online directory that lists various Rosa Parks Web sites from all over the Internet. Included are links to biographies, awards, newspaper articles, book reviews, and more. A great place to get started looking for more information about the "Mother of the Civil Rights Movement."

ABOUT THE AUTHOR

Chuck Bednar is an author and freelance writer from Ohio. He has been writing professionally since 1997 and has written more than 1,500 published nonfiction articles. Furthermore, Bednar is the author of eight books, including the *Tony Parker* and *Tim Duncan* entries in Mason Crest's MODERN ROLE MODELS series, as well as SUPERSTARS OF PRO FOOTBALL: *Tony Romo*. He is currently employed by Bright Hub (www.brighthub.com) as the Managing Editor for their Nintendo Wii Web site.